THE GOLDEN BOOK
BELFAST

Text by
ALAN MORROW

Photos by
ANDREA FANTAUZZO

O'BRIEN
DUBLIN

BONECHI

CONTENTS

History of Belfast

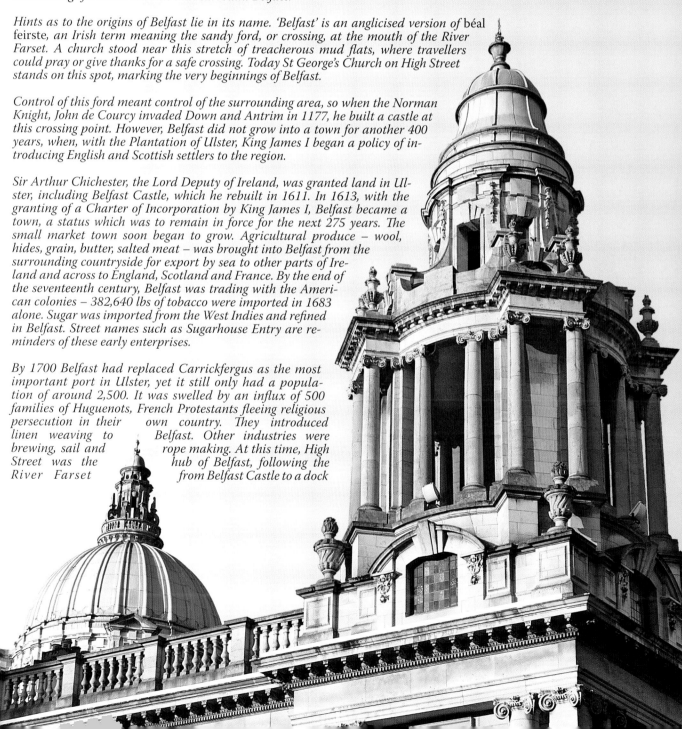

*B*elfast has a history of settlement that dates back over four hundred years, so while it may be an old city, it is not an ancient one. However, there is ample historical proof to show that people have been drawn to the broad flood plains of the River Lagan for thousands of years. The Giant's Ring, an enormous 5,000 year old henge, or earthwork circle, on the outskirts of the city, is impressive evidence of Neolithic man's activities in the area. Elsewhere, the remains of numerous Iron Age forts dot the hills that surround Belfast.

Hints as to the origins of Belfast lie in its name. 'Belfast' is an anglicised version of *béal feirste, an Irish term meaning the sandy ford, or crossing, at the mouth of the River Farset. A church stood near this stretch of treacherous mud flats, where travellers could pray or give thanks for a safe crossing. Today St George's Church on High Street stands on this spot, marking the very beginnings of Belfast.

Control of this ford meant control of the surrounding area, so when the Norman Knight, John de Courcy invaded Down and Antrim in 1177, he built a castle at this crossing point. However, Belfast did not grow into a town for another 400 years, when, with the Plantation of Ulster, King James I began a policy of introducing English and Scottish settlers to the region.

Sir Arthur Chichester, the Lord Deputy of Ireland, was granted land in Ulster, including Belfast Castle, which he rebuilt in 1611. In 1613, with the granting of a Charter of Incorporation by King James I, Belfast became a town, a status which was to remain in force for the next 275 years. The small market town soon began to grow. Agricultural produce – wool, hides, grain, butter, salted meat – was brought into Belfast from the surrounding countryside for export by sea to other parts of Ireland and across to England, Scotland and France. By the end of the seventeenth century, Belfast was trading with the American colonies – 382,640 lbs of tobacco were imported in 1683 alone. Sugar was imported from the West Indies and refined in Belfast. Street names such as Sugarhouse Entry are reminders of these early enterprises.

By 1700 Belfast had replaced Carrickfergus as the most important port in Ulster, yet it still only had a population of around 2,500. It was swelled by an influx of 500 families of Huguenots, French Protestants fleeing religious persecution in their own country. They introduced linen weaving to Belfast. Other industries were brewing, sail and rope making. At this time, High Street was the hub of Belfast, following the River Farset from Belfast Castle to a dock

where it joined the River Lagan. There were just two prominent buildings: Belfast Castle and the Parish Church, which stood on the site of the present day St George's Church.

Linen had a profound effect on the growth and wealth of Belfast. Increasing amounts were exported from Belfast throughout the eighteenth century: 200,000 yards were exported in 1701, which had risen to 17 million yards by 1773. A Harbour Board was set up in 1785 to address urgently needed improvements to the port, and in line with this, a fledgling shipbuilding industry began in 1791. The 1800s saw unparalleled industrial growth. By 1873 Belfast was the largest linen producing centre in the world, a position it held until 1914, and its vast, noisy, damp mills employed thousands. The mighty Harland & Wolff shipyard came into being in 1861. The company is best known for building the ill-fated RMS Titanic. Today Harland & Wolff's two magnificent yellow twin cranes, Goliath and Samson, built in 1969 and 1974 respectively, stand sentinel over the city.

Belfast's industrial wealth created some of its finest Victorian buildings. The Harbour Commissioners Office opened in 1854 and the Custom House in 1857. The Albert Memorial Clock was completed in 1869. However, with the granting of city status by Queen Victoria in 1888, a decision was taken to build a new City Hall using profits from the Belfast Gasworks, for which Belfast Corporation (now Belfast City Council) had responsibility. Thus Belfast City Hall came into being, the architectural gem in the city's crown.

The twentieth century marked a period of political change in Belfast and throughout Northern Ireland. The Government of Ireland Act 1920 provided for two separate Home Rule territories in Ireland. The Act partitioned the country into Northern Ireland, which established the Parliament of Northern Ireland, and Southern Ireland, where the Act was not implemented. From 1921 until 1932, the Parliament of Northern Ireland found a temporary home in Assembly's College (now Union Theological College) in Botanic Avenue, Belfast. Thereafter it moved to the newly built Parliament Buildings at Stormont, in the east of the city.

Much of Belfast's more recent history has been characterised by political unrest and community strife. Fortunately, the country has now entered a more settled phase and Belfast is a city reborn. The Victoria Shopping Centre, which opened in 2008, is at the centre of its booming shopping scene. Other buildings, such as the Waterfront Hall concert venue and the Odyssey entertainment complex, are bold statements of civic pride. Visitors from every continent throng its streets, soaking up the atmosphere of a city with heart.

Left: Albert Memorial Clock, completed in 1869.
Below and right: Belfast Castle.

Location

Belfast is situated on the north-east coast of Ireland, at the western end of Belfast Lough and the mouth of the River Lagan nestled between a series of hills, including Cave Hill, which is thought to have been the inspiration for Jonathan Swift's novel *Gulliver's Travels* (its profile suggests a giant lying in repose).

Belfast has excellent transport facilities. The modern George Best Belfast City Airport is only ten minutes from the city centre and serves all main UK and European cities. Alternatively, Belfast International Airport at Aldergrove is less than thirty minutes away via the M2 motorway. Central Train Station has excellent links with Northern Ireland's other main cities and towns, as well as regular Enterprise train services to Dublin. There are also first-rate ferry services from the Port of Belfast to Scotland and England.

For any visitor wishing to explore the city, Belfast Welcome Centre in the City Centre, is the ideal starting point. Visitors will find everything they need to know about planning a stay in the city, with help from friendly, experienced staff who know Belfast intimately. Whether it's Pub Tours, Titanic Trails, Christian Heritage, Art Galleries, tracing one's genealogy or finding accommodation, help is always at hand in the Belfast Welcome Centre.

Belfast Welcome Centre
T: +44 (0)28 9023 9026
E: info@belfastvisitor.com
W: www.gotobelfast.com

Belfast today

Belfast. As with all great cities, a river runs through it. Attractive walkways with eye-catching public art line the banks of the River Lagan, and everywhere there is the buzz of people relaxing at street-side cafes, enjoying fine restaurants or soaking up the atmosphere of a place that is at ease with itself. Every visitor can be a part of this scene and because Belfast is so compact, it is easy to explore on foot.

Over the years Belfast has evolved into a city of distinct quarters, each of which has its own character and charm, formed from history, architecture and chance. The Victorian era was probably the most influential in terms of defining and shaping the city as it is today. This was the period of Belfast's full industrial might, when linen weaving, rope making, engineering and trade made the city one of the great powerhouses of the Victorian age.

One Victorian architect, more than any other, has left an indelible and quite remarkable stamp on Belfast's architectural heritage. Many of the city's most imposing buildings were designed by Sir Charles Lanyon, to the extent that Belfast is sometimes referred to as 'Lanyon City'. Great buildings such as Queen's University, the Custom House, Belfast Public Library, even the County Courthouse and Gaol, all bear the hallmarks of his confident style. Today these are interspersed with other constructions from earlier and later periods and it is this seemingly haphazard, but honest mix of styles and periods that lends such charm and integrity to the Belfast streetscape.

Visitors staying in the city centre will be able to savour city living to the full. The Victorian splendour of St George's Market is only a short walk from the city centre and it is a great place to get a real taste of Belfast. Weekly markets are held there, offering the freshest food from Northern Ireland and beyond, and St George's regularly hosts festive events, design and craft fairs, exhibitions and concerts.

Opposite page: Europa Hotel, Belfast Welcome Centre, Public Art.
This page: May Street.

The Waterfront Hall in Lanyon Place is directly opposite St George's Market. This is Belfast's leading concert hall and is a must-see destination for all lovers of live music. Also nearby is the city's newest open air public forum, Custom House Square. It spreads before the Italianate splendour of the Custom House and hosts a heady programme of concerts, festivals and public events. Ireland's premier entertainment venue, the Odyssey, is only a short walk from the city centre, with a mix of restaurants, bars and cinemas that offers something for all ages and tastes. Then there is the wedding cake spectacle of the City Hall, in the heart of the City Centre area. Its grounds make the ideal setting for an al fresco lunch and there are guided tours of its sumptuous interior.

Cathedral Quarter, the area centred round St Anne's Cathedral, is the oldest part of Belfast. It offers all sorts of intriguing possibilities, with cobbled lanes and alleys leading to imposing Victorian architecture, snug pubs, trendy bars and chic restaurants. Towards the south of the city is Queen's

Top: St Anne's Cathedral.
Left: Waterfront Hall.
Right: The Custom House.

Quarter, with the magnificent Lanyon Building of Queen's University. Queen's Quarter is distinct from any other part of Belfast, with an atmosphere and charm of its own. Verdant and full of trees, it has the great green lung of Botanic Gardens at its heart. But this is a university area, so it is the young people of Queen's Quarter whose vitality and lust for life give it a real zing.

Belfast also has its own Gaeltacht Quarter, or Irish-speaking quarter, focused on the people and communities of the Falls Road. This part of west Belfast is the hub of Belfast's vibrant and fast growing Irish language community. At its heart is the Irish cultural centre, Cultúrlann Mc Adam Ó Fiaich. Located in a former Presbyterian church, An Cultúrlann's cosmopolitan atmosphere and its reputation for excellent food, have made it an established meeting place for international travellers and backpackers, as well as celebrities visiting Belfast.

Left: Café Vaudeville, City Centre.
Below right: Enjoying a pint in the Crown Bar.
Below: The Lanyon Building, Queen's University.

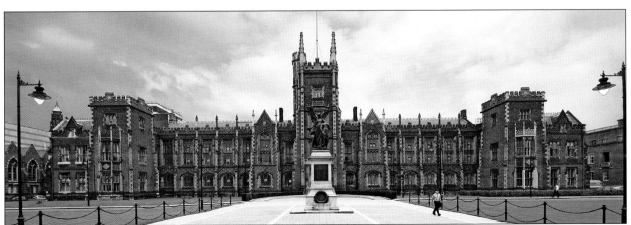

City Centre

Belfast City Centre is the heart of a busy, thriving urban metropolis that owes its origins to the town's industrial growth in the nineteenth century. The granting of city-status by Queen Victoria in 1888, emboldened Belfast's proud citizens to build a magnificent City Hall that would reflect their city's power and prestige.

Eight years later, in 1906, Belfast City Hall opened and today it presents a perfect expression of the prosperity and civic pride of the city at the turn of the nineteenth century. It also remains one of the most important examples of the Classical Renaissance style anywhere in the British Isles.

Life in the city was not all formality. Belfast folk of the past certainly knew how to enjoy themselves too. Exotic palaces of entertainment such as the Grand Opera House, the Ulster Hall and, of course, the famous Crown Bar show that its citizens enjoyed good music, comedy, drama and perhaps the occasional drink, as indeed they still do to this day.

City Hall

The best place to start a tour of Belfast is the City Hall. In 1888 Queen Victoria granted Belfast the status of City and in response its citizens built the magnificent City Hall, which today dominates the heart of Belfast. A Public Architectural Competition was held, from which the design of a young London architect, Alfred Brumwell Thomas, was selected. Set in attractive public gardens, the City Hall is built in the Classical Renaissance style in Portland stone and Italian marble. Its rectangular shape encloses a quadrangle courtyard. It opened in 1906, at a cost of £360,000, the funds for which came from the profits of the Belfast Gasworks.

Visitors to the City Hall are welcomed by the grandest of entrances. The impressive stone porte-cochere leads through to the marble-lined octagonal vestibule, then into a magnificent entrance hall with grand staircase, featuring four types of marble. The intricately decorated principal dome soars overhead to a height of approximately 53 metres (173 feet). The Rotunda creates a circular viewing gallery looking down on the Entrance Hall. The building features a number of grand rooms. Belfast City Council sits in the Council Chamber on the first

Opposite: The Ulster Hall.
Right: Statue of Queen Victoria, Belfast City Hall.
Below: Belfast City Hall.

Above left: The City Hall from Donegall Place.
Above right: City Hall entrance and front façade.
Below: The porte-cochere, Belfast City Hall.

working day of each month. It contains many notable portraits, including King Edward VII by Harold Speed; Queen Victoria, Sir Edward Harland and Sir Robert Coey, by Sir Thomas Jones; Sir Robert Anderson by Henrietta Rae; and the Earl of Shaftesbury by Sir John Lavery.

The Great Hall was almost totally destroyed by a German air raid on the night of 4 May 1941. Fortunately, its seven magnificent stained glass windows had already been removed for safekeeping. They were reinstated after the war when the Hall was rebuilt and restored to its former grandeur.

Among the many noteworthy statues in its grounds is the marble figure of 'Thane' on a granite pedestal, sculpted by Sir Thomas Brock. Unveiled in 1920, it commemorates the sinking of the *RMS Titanic* in 1912. The Belfast War Memorial, designed by Alfred Brumwell Thomas and unveiled on Armistice Day 1929, takes the form of a Greek Cenotaph with the background of a colonnade.

Belfast City Hall has played a central role in many of the city's historic events. It was the seat of Northern Ireland's first parliament after partition in 1921, and has been the focus of huge rallies and demonstrations, such as the VE Day celebrations in 1945. It has

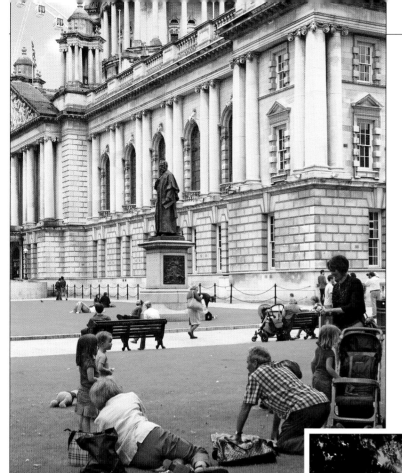

hosted welcomes for Olympic gold medallist Mary Peters, world boxing champion Barry McGuigan, and President Bill Clinton of the United States of America. There are regular tours of the City Hall and its grounds. Details are available at the reception desk in the main foyer or at the Belfast Welcome Centre in the City Centre.

Above left: Relaxing in the grounds of Belfast City Hall.
Above right: The Belfast War Memorial at the City Hall.
Right: The City Hall at night.

Linen Hall Library

The Linen Hall Library stands on Donegall Square North, opposite the City Hall. It is the oldest library in Belfast and the last subscribing library in Ireland. Founded in 1788 as the Belfast Reading Society, it took a particular interest in the natural, civil, commercial and ecclesiastical history of Ireland, an impetus that remains to this day. The library was originally housed in the White Linen Hall, on the site of the present day City Hall. However, the present building, a linen warehouse built in the 1860s, was purchased in 1888. Today, the Linen Hall Library houses one of the most renowned collections of Irish material in the world. It is the centre for 'Irish and Local Studies' in the north of Ireland and its holdings range from its comprehensive stock of 'Early Belfast and Ulster' printed books to the 250,000 items in the 'Northern Ireland Political Collection', the definitive archive of the recent troubles. Visitors are always welcome to browse through its collections. Free tours are available throughout the year by prior booking.

Above: The Linen Hall Library.
Right: Inside the Linen Hall Library.

The Crown Bar

The Crown Liquor Saloon, or Crown Bar as it is better known, is an architectural gem, a priceless time capsule and one of the city's most celebrated pubs. Not only does it capture the opulence of the Victorian era, but it remains a real pub, enjoyed by locals and visitors alike, where the drama of life in the city is played out every day. The Crown Bar was built in 1826 as the rather nondescript Railway Tavern. However, in the 1880s it was taken over by Michael Flanagan. His son Patrick, inspired by architecture he had seen in Spain and Italy, drew up ambitious plans for the Crown's advancement. At that time, Ireland was awash with craftsmen from all over Europe who were helping to build new churches. The Flanagans hired Italian craftsmen to turn their grand designs into reality. The results were unveiled in 1885 and the Crown's opulent stained glass, ornate plaster mouldings, push button bells, detailed tile work and intricately carved snugs caused an immediate stir. The 1960s and 1970s were not kind to the Crown. Its location opposite the Europa Hotel, the most bombed hotel in Europe, caused it to be buffeted by more than forty blasts. Fortunately, when the National Trust assumed ownership in 1978, their extensive restoration returned the bar to its full Victorian splendour. Today, the Crown's opulent interior still impresses visitors from around the world.

High Street

This was Belfast's earliest main street. Troops paraded down here from Belfast Castle, hence its original name, 'Grand Parade'. No trace remains of the castle, but the upper end of High Street is still known as Castle Place. In the 1600s and 1700s, the River Farset flowed down the middle of High Street and over time, its banks became the quaysides of a thriving town and trading port. Echoes of the sea faring past can be found all around in the names of streets, such as Skipper Street, and in pub names: the Mermaid Inn at Wilson's Court; the Morning Star in Pottinger's Entry and the Crow's Nest in Skipper Street.

Right: Pottinger's Entry.
Below: Cave Hill.
Below (inset): Jonathan Swift.

Jonathan Swift

The Irish born satirist, Jonathan Swift, 1667–1745, lived in nearby Waring Street. Cave Hill, which overlooks Belfast, is said to have given him inspiration for *Gulliver's Travels*, because its outline resembles a giant lying in repose.

Grand Opera House

The Grand Opera House opened its doors to an expectant public on 23 December 1895, and from the outset it was a success. Crowds flocked to see a variety of entertainment, including opera, drama, pantomime and the latest London comedies or musicals.

Since then, the Grand Opera House has given stage to many great names from the world of entertainment. In 1963 a young Luciano Pavarotti made his UK debut there, as Lieutenant Pinkerton in a production of *Madame Butterfly*.

The Grand Opera House was designed by the leading theatre architect, Frank Matcham, and it is a glorious expression of the skills of Victorian architects, painters and craftsmen. The elephants' heads and intricate plasterwork on the front of the two balconies give the auditorium a distinctly Indian theme. It is richly decorated throughout with gold leaf.

This national treasure was used as a cinema for over twenty years from 1950, and was closed and boarded up in 1972. Fortunately, following a campaign by the Ulster Architectural Heritage Society, it was granted listed status and its survival was assured.

Right: Belfast's Grand Opera House.

The long process of restoration began in 1975 and re-opening night took place on 15 September 1980. However, the building's trials were not yet over and it suffered bomb damage in 1991 and 1993, which was swiftly repaired. Today the Grand Opera House continues to present a programme of the very best in live theatrical performances and plays host to companies from around the world.

St George's Market

Completed in 1896, St George's Market was the supermarket of its day, a place where people came to buy eggs, butter, poultry, fruit and vegetables. There were once many such markets in Belfast but St George's Market is the only surviving example. In addition to its role as a food market, St George's is a lively retail, cultural and conference venue. Visitors are welcome to its weekly food markets and it regularly hosts such events as fashion shows, boxing tournaments and exhibitions.

Opposite: Ornate entrance to St George's Market.
Above: Antiques and collectables for sale at St George's Market.
Below: The finest fresh food and local produce at St George's Market.

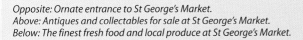

Waterfront Hall

In 1997, five years after it was first conceived, Belfast's magnificent Waterfront Hall opened for business on Lanyon Place. The city has a real sense of pride in this splendid, glass fronted, pleasure dome, which appears to float on the River Lagan.

The Waterfront Hall is one of the architectural stars of the city and it sits effortlessly among the Victorian buildings of Belfast's skyline. Its superb circular auditorium, which has a seating capacity of 2,235, has witnessed performances of every taste and style: from rock, opera, ballet and classical music, to pantomime and stand-up comedy. Some intriguing public art is located around the Waterfront Hall. 'Barrel Man' sits astride a barrel of beer and on the open plaza to the front of the hall, 'Sheep on the Road' reflects the site's history as the largest sheep and cattle market in Belfast.

The Waterfront Hall, perhaps more than any other contemporary building, encapsulates Belfast's vision for its future and is an expression of its confidence as a modern, progressive European city.

Above: The Waterfront Hall's circular auditorium.
Below: The Waterfront Hall and River Lagan.

St George's Church

There are records of a chapel at *béal feirste* (Irish for 'the sandy ford at the mouth of the Farset') going back almost 1,000 years. A small chapel belonging to the Church of Sancles (Shankill) stood here. It was used by pilgrims waiting to cross the mud flats, which were dangerous at high tide. Here they could pray to have a safe crossing of the River Farset.

This site is steeped in history. Oliver Cromwell stationed his troops here and used lead from the roof of the church to make musket shot. King William III attended a service at the church on 15 June 1690 while on his way to the Battle of the Boyne. The oak chair in which he sat is still in use.

The present church is a large and elegant Georgian building designed by John Bowden of Dublin and completed in 1816.

Right: St George's Church (interior).
Below: St George's Church (exterior).

Above: Detail of May Street Presbyterian Church.
Below: The classically Georgian proportions of May Street Presbyterian Church.

Cornmarket

Cornmarket is a short street running from Castle Place to Arthur Square. It played a poignant role in the history of Belfast and Ireland, as the place where Henry Joy Mc-Cracken, one of Belfast's most prominent citizens, and leader of the United Irishmen, was hanged on 17 July 1798. McCracken had led a band of rebels in the Battle of Antrim and was caught following their defeat. After his trial at the Assembly Rooms, he was taken for execution to Cornmarket, on gallows erected outside the Market House. The Market House had been built in 1639 as the main public hall of the town, on land that had originally been given to the town by McCracken's great great grandfather. Buried at first in St George's graveyard, his body was later re-interred at Clifton Street graveyard.

St Malachy's Church

A short distance from the City Hall, on Adelaide Street, stands St Malachy's Church. This fine castellated Eliza-bethan-Gothic style church, surely one of the most romantic buildings in Belfast, was designed by Thomas Jackson. The building was consecrated by the primate Dr Crolly in 1844. Its castle-like exterior is complete with turrets and arrow slits. The studded doors open onto an incredible interior with an impressive gallery. The wonderful fan-vaulted ceiling, like an inside-out wedding cake, is an imitation of Henry VII's Westminster Abbey chapel. The church organ, installed by the famous Telford family of Dublin, is one of the most important instruments in Ulster. In 1868, the largest bell turret in Belfast was added to the church. The bell was taken away shortly afterwards, due to complaints that its deafening noise was interfering with the maturing of the whiskey in nearby Dunville's distillery.

May Street Presbyterian Church

This magnificent classical Georgian church has been in continuous use since it opened in 1829. It displays the restrained elegance that is born of good proportion and scale and, as with other buildings of this period, it was designed to honour and enhance the developing town of Belfast. Designed by William Smith and built by John Brown, the imposing steps of the main frontage lead up to two Ionic style columns and four pilasters, 8.5 metres high (28 feet), surmounted by a beautiful pediment. Inside, the vestibule is dominated by the Cooke Memorial doorway, which takes the form of a miniature classical Triumphal Arch. Symmetrical stone staircases lead up to the spacious gallery, supported on cast iron columns. The front of the gallery is elegantly panelled in mahogany. The church is an oasis of calm in the heart of the city.

Presbyterian Assembly Buildings

This impressive three-storey building at the junction of Fisherwick Place, Great Victoria Street, Howard Street and Grosvenor Road, is the headquarters for the Presbyterian Church in Ireland. Its Gothic architecture is loosely styled on the architecture of a Scottish baronial castle. The building was opened in 1905 by the Duke of Argyll and its tower, which houses Belfast's only peal of twelve bells, is modelled on that of St Giles's Cathedral in Edinburgh. At the heart of the building is the large D-shaped Assembly Hall, one of the most impressive interiors in Belfast.

Above: Royal Belfast Academical Institution, or 'Inst'.

Entered on the first floor, it has seating for 1,300 and is noted for its two tiers of galleries and a great oblong roof light with coloured glass of art nouveau pattern.

Royal Belfast Academical Institution

Royal Belfast Academical Institution, or Inst., occupies a 3.2 hectares site (8 acres) in the centre of Belfast. The eminent English architect John Soane, who designed the new Bank of England in 1788, drew up plans for the school in 1809 and its foundation stone was laid in July 1810. The building was formally opened at 1.00pm on 1 February 1814. Among the many renowned pupils to have passed through Royal Belfast Academical Institution was Thomas Andrews, born 1873, the Chief Designer of *RMS Titanic* and nephew to Lord William Pirrie who owned Harland and Wolff shipyard where the ship was built. Andrews was a much respected figure in the shipyard. He went down with the vessel when it sank after striking an iceberg on its maiden voyage in 1912.

Pubs and Bars
in the City Centre

The Garrick Bar
29 Chichester Street

Wine and spirits have been dispensed here since 1870. Sensitively restored in recent years, The Garrick's traditional gas-lit exterior forms a welcoming beacon in the city, while inside, it features high ceilings, delicate woodwork and exquisite tiling. This pub's easy-going ambience and city centre location make it a popular spot.

Robinson's
38 Great Victoria Street

One of the Belfast's most renowned drinking emporia, Robinson's houses five very different venues in a large Victorian building. Traditionalists will err towards the mahogany and mirrors of the Saloon Bar or the spit and sawdust ambience of Fibber Magees. For a more contemporary experience, try BT1, The Bistro or the Roxy. There's truly something for everyone at Robinson's.

Bittles Bar
70 Upper Church Lane

This compact and comfortable pub, squeezed into the apex of a triangular Victorian building, is a popular venue for people of all ages, from old hands studying the current racing form, to young go-getters popping in for a swift drink. Serves classic Belfast pub grub.

Shopping in Belfast
City Centre

Victoria Square

This 'must visit' destination is Northern Ireland's biggest, brightest, newest shopping centre. Four floors of fantastic stores, great places to eat and drink, an eight screen Odeon cinema and House of Fraser department store. Crowning it all is the dazzling glass dome and viewing gallery, with 360° of 'wow' over Belfast.

1 Victoria Square

Castlecourt
Royal Avenue

If you're looking for great fashion, homeware, beauty, footwear, jewellery, toys and much more, then head for Castlecourt shopping centre. As well as great shopping, thoughtful touches such as a dedicated customer service desk, soft play area and free kiddie car hire will make your experience as stress-free as possible.

Howard Street
Upper Queen Street
Wellington Street

Howard Street
Upper Queen Street
Wellington Street

For an intimate shopping experience, this area is chock-full of exquisite outlets offering everything from designer fashion and bespoke jewellery, to lifestyle homeware and fine food. Make sure to visit this area for some of the very best shopping in Belfast.

Queen's Arcade
Donegall Place

A stroll through this ornate 1880s shopping arcade will take you past numerous intriguing, independent shops, as well as Belfast's most prestigious jewellers. Queen's Arcade leads into Fountain Street, with many great coffee shops, gift stores, a book store and outlets selling local crafts.

Rosemary Street First Presbyterian Church

Situated just off the busy shopping thoroughfare of Royal Avenue, First Presbyterian Church on Rosemary Street is Belfast's oldest surviving place of worship within the old town boundary. The present building was designed by Roger Mulholland and built 1781–1783 at a cost of £2,300. John Wesley, 1703–1791, founder of the 'Methodist revival', preached here in 1789 and wrote in his journal that 'It is the completest place of worship I have ever seen....beautiful in the highest degree.' Noted for its unusual oval shape, the interior has intricate wooden carving, as well as notable stained glass windows and traditional box pews. The 1922 First World War Memorial is by the noted County Down sculptor, Rosamund Praeger. The church survived four bombings in the 1970s and still has an active congregation.

Below: Rosemary Street First Presbyterian Church.

The Ulster Hall

Situated on Bedford Street, behind the City Hall, the Ulster Hall has brought spectacle and delight to the people of Belfast since 1862. It was built at a time when the city was attracting major artists and needed a bigger concert hall. Its organ was presented to the people of Belfast by a former Lord Mayor, Mr Andrew Mulholland, at a reputed cost of 3,000 guineas. The Mulholland Grand Organ, as it is known, was rebuilt in 1903 and completely restored between 1976 and 1978. It remains one of the oldest and finest examples of classical English organ-building being played today.

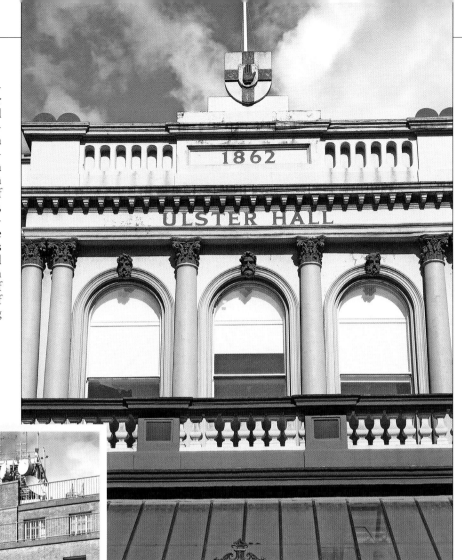

BBC Broadcasting House

Broadcasting House on Ormeau Avenue is the home of the BBC in Northern Ireland. Designed in 1936 by James Millar of Glasgow, its imposing and austere neo-Georgian style is typical of the era.

The BBC began its operations in 1924, working from a disused linen warehouse in Linen Hall Street but in 1938 work began on the new building and in May 1941 Broadcasting House was officially opened. It contained a spacious concert hall, and several studios, all of which were used for radio broadcasts. The first television output in Northern Ireland began in 1953, timed so that viewers could witness the Coronation of Queen Elizabeth II.

Top: The Ulster Hall.
Left: BBC Broadcasting House.

Cathedral Quarter

Cathedral Quarter occupies a distinctive site which marks the very origins of Belfast. Public works regularly unearth evidence of the sixteenth and seventeenth century industrial life of this area. Recent finds include pot houses (pots), tanneries (leather), coopers (barrel makers) and slaughterhouses. These echoes of the past are reflected in the buildings and street layouts that give Cathedral Quarter its unique character.

Cathedral Quarter is full of fascinating architecture, ranging from ostentatious banks and public buildings, to cosy pubs and trendy warehouse restaurants. Some of these occupy prominent public locations. But there are other equally intriguing buildings to be discovered down the narrow cobbled streets and alleyways that give the area its intimate charm.

In recent years, Cathedral Quarter has taken on a pivotal role as the focus for Belfast's burgeoning arts and crafts scene. It is home to many visual and dramatic artists, as well as community groups, and each year it hosts the internationally acclaimed Cathedral Quarter Arts Festival.

St Anne's Cathedral

St Anne's Cathedral is at the very heart of Cathedral Quarter and gives the area its name. When Queen Victoria made Belfast a City in 1888, it was decided to build a new cathedral on the site of the existing St Anne's Parish Church, founded in 1776. Designs were drawn up in the Hiberno-Romanesque style by the Irish architect, Sir Thomas Drew and the foundation stone was laid in 1899. The waterlogged ground on which it was built meant that the new building required extensive piling up to a depth of 15 metres (50 feet). Work continued over the next eighty years, with the construction of the Baptistry in 1928 and the Chapel of the Holy Spirit in 1932. Work on the Eastern Apse and Ambulatory commenced in 1955, and ten years later work began on the transepts. The North Transept was completed in 1981.

The walls of the building are of Somerset stone, with an inner lining of Dumfries sandstone. The roof timbers are Australian sequoia and the

Right and below: The dramatic interior of St Anne's Cathedral.

wooden floor of the nave is Canadian maple. The aisles are floored with Irish marble. Entrance is through the deeply recessed Great West Door and inside, the floor is laid out as a black and white marble maze. Follow the black path, representing sin, to a dead end, or follow the white path to the sanctuary, the heart of the church.

The pillars of the nave are each crowned with capitals representing different aspects of life in and around the city, such as womanhood and shipbuilding. The ceiling of the Baptistry is of particular interest. It contains over 150,000 pieces of glass which represent earth, air, fire and water, hence symbolising Creation. The Gothic pulpit, a gift from Westminster Abbey, was felt to be too ornate and was replaced by a modern pulpit in 1959. The original was unfortunately lost in a fire. The cathedral contains only one tomb, Lord Carson of Duncairn, buried here in 1935 by virtue of a special Act of Parliament.

Left: St Anne's Cathedral (interior).
Below: Detail of main entrance, St Anne's Cathedral.
Opposite: St Anne's Cathedral, showing the Spire of Hope.

In April 2007 a stainless steel spire was installed on top of the cathedral. Named the 'Spire of Hope', it is illuminated at night. It rises some 40 metres (131 feet) in height and the base section protrudes through a glass platform in the Cathedral's roof directly above the choir stalls, allowing visitors to view it from the nave.

Opposite St Anne's Cathedral is an open area of public space called Writers' Square. It pays homage to Belfast's rich literary tradition, with quotations about Belfast by famous local writers carved into the stone underfoot. Visitors enjoy seeing how many writers' names and inscriptions they can find.

Above right, Writers' Square, Belfast.

Clifton Street Burying Ground

Clifton Street Burying Ground opened in March 1797 as a non-denominational graveyard in the grounds of Clifton House, in North Queen Street, at the upper end of Donegall Street. It was established by the Belfast Charitable Society to generate income through the sale of plots, and to provide an additional burial ground for Belfast's growing population. The most pitiful part of the graveyard is a large space in the upper portion called 'Strangers' Ground'. This is the last resting place of thousands of victims of disease (typhus, cholera, dysentery, smallpox) and famine that broke out in Belfast in the mid 1800s. A simple stone memorial marks the plot. Nearby lie some of the city's most influential, and infamous, sons and daughters. Famous names such as Heron (founder of the Ulster Bank), Ritchie (shipbuilder), Dunville (whiskey distiller), Ewart (linen) and Drummond (medicine), lie alongside those of Henry Joy McCracken (leader of the United Irishmen) and his sister, Mary Ann McCracken (member of the Society of United Irishmen and social reformer).

Clifton Street Orange Hall

The Grand Orange Lodge, or Orange Order, is a Protestant fraternity with members throughout the world. Clifton Street Orange Hall (1883–1885), is the work of the architect William Batt. The building was originally intended to be unobtrusive. However, it features one of the most eye-catching adornments in Belfast – a three metres (10 feet) high equestrian statue of King William III of Orange, the triumphant figure of 1690. Cast in bronze by Harry Hems of Exeter, it was unveiled in 1889.

Left: Clifton Street Burying Ground.

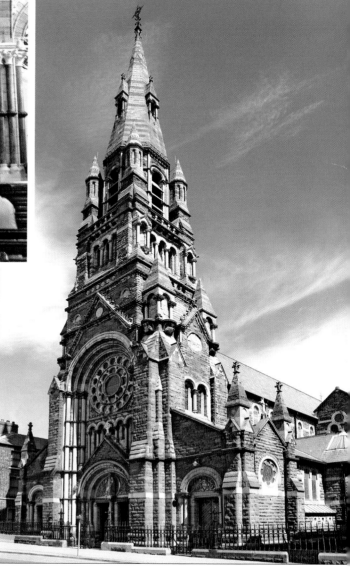

St Patrick's Church.

St Patrick's Church

St Patrick's Church on Donegall Street opened on 12 August 1877. Designed by Timothy Hevey, it is modelled on SS Augustine & John on Thomas Street, Dublin and is built in Romanesque style, with beautiful arches of red sandstone supported on slender grey and rose Dumfries granite pillars. The interior of the roof is sheeted in pitch pine and a 2 ton (2.03 tonnes) bronze bell is located in the tower which, together with the spire and cross, rises to a height of 54.8 metres (180 feet). The side chapel contains a triptych of St Patrick, the Madonna and St Bridget, known as 'The Madonna of the Lakes'. It was presented to the church by the renowned society painter, Sir John Lavery, in memory of his baptism in the original St Patrick's Church. The face of the Madonna is that of his wife Hazel, the famous society hostess.

Belfast Harbour Office

For over 150 years, the Harbour Office in Corporation Square has been the headquarters of the Belfast Harbour Commissioners, the body responsible for the operation of the Port of Belfast. It opened in 1854 and incorporates a conspicuous clock tower that was used to regulate the punctual sailing of passenger steamers. It is sumptuously decorated, inside and out. Of particular interest are the marble floors in the ground floor reception area and in the first floor lobby. Also noteworthy are the stained glass windows depicting industry, commerce and enterprise, together with the coats of arms of the many ports and cities with which Belfast traded in the past. Belfast Harbour Office has seen many notable visitors over the years, including Queen Victoria (1849), King George VI and Queen Elizabeth (1945), and Queen Elizabeth II and Duke of Edinburgh (1961).

Right: Belfast Harbour Office.
Below: The Custom House.

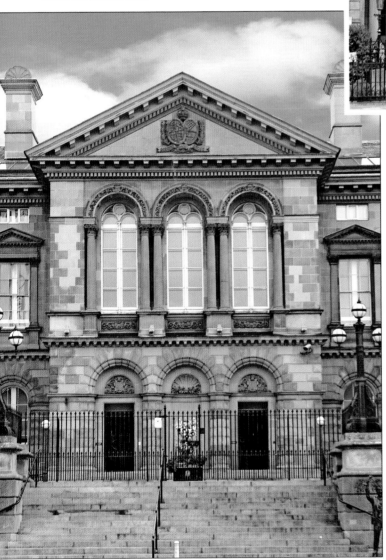

Sinclair Seamen's Presbyterian Church

This is one of the most idiosyncratic and charming churches in Belfast. Consecrated in 1857, it was erected in memory of John Sinclair and designed by Charles Lanyon. Built in a rather unusual L-shape, it is Venetian in style, as signified by the Square Tower and 'Rialto Bridge' archway. The church was built to serve the spiritual needs of sailors coming into Belfast's busy port and its interior has a distinctly nautical theme. A large brass wheel and a capstan form the centre pieces to the church. They come from a ship that sank off the coast of Scotland in the First World War. A brass bell from the warship, *HMS Hood*, is rung every Sunday at the start of the evening service. Even the collection plates are in the shape of lifeboats.

Custom House

The Custom House is an imposing two storey Victorian building designed by Charles Lanyon and built in the Italianate style. Completed in 1857, the building originally housed the Custom Service, as well as the General Post Office, Inland Revenue, the Stamp Offices and Government Emigration Departments. It is worth circling the Custom House to take in its full splendour, notably the lofty pediment to the front, with Britan-

nia, Mercury and Neptune gazing out over Belfast harbour, carved by the acclaimed stonemason, Thomas Fitzpatrick. The leading English writer Anthony Trollope (1815–1882) worked for the General Post Office in the Custom House for several years. As well as being a renowned novelist, Trollope also invented the pillar-box.

Custom House Square

Custom House Square, the open area in front of the Custom House, is a popular public space where people can meet, socialise and be entertained. Custom House Square has a long history as a public arena. In the nineteenth and early twentieth centuries it was Belfast's 'Speakers' Corner' and large crowds regularly gathered at the foot of the Custom House steps to hear and heckle the orators of the day. This history is celebrated today by 'The Speaker', a life size bronze statue standing on the steps. The large lights that fringe the square are aptly named 'The Hecklers'.

Above: The water feature at Custom House Square.
Below: The Custom House and Bigfish.

Pubs and Bars
in Cathedral Quarter

McHugh's
29-31 Queen's Square

Built nearly 300 years ago, McHugh's occupies one of the oldest buildings in Belfast and proudly displays its original handmade bricks and massive eighteenth-century oak trusses. With great atmosphere, fine food and grand pints, and set on the fringe of Custom House Square, McHugh's is at the very heart of the Cathedral Quarter.

The John Hewitt Bar
51 Donegall Street

Named in honour of the free-thinking Belfast poet, The John Hewitt is not only an ideal place to meet and socialise, it also pours some of the best real ales in the city and puts on live music, ranging from jazz and blues to folk and traditional. This is a pub where conversation is cherished, so there's no intrusive juke box or canned music to spoil your enjoyment of the craic.

Kelly's Cellars
30 Bank Street

Once a country pub on the edge of town, Kelly's Cellars is the oldest continually run pub in Belfast. Throughout its history, it has remained an everyday drinking man's pub, where an eclectic mix of Belfast characters – artists, writers and actors – gather to sup pints of Guinness and discuss the ways of the world. There's never a dull moment in Kelly's.

Above: Custom House Square at night (inset: 'The Speaker').
Below left: Albert Memorial Clock.
Below right: The Lagan Weir.

Albert Memorial Clock

The Albert Memorial Clock, one of Belfast's best loved landmarks, is affectionately known as the city's very own 'leaning tower'. Over the years subsidence at its foundations has caused the clock to adopt a lean some distance from vertical. It was built as a memorial to Queen Victoria's husband, Prince Albert, who died in 1861. The clock has been the centrepiece of many historical events – one enterprising young lad is said to have scaled its very summit in order to get a better view of the launch of *RMS Titanic* from the Harland & Wolff shipyard.

The Lagan Weir

The River Lagan is the city's greatest asset, but for many years it was neglected and polluted. The process of change and improvement started in 1994, when the Laganside Corporation built the Lagan Weir. It is used to control the flow of water in the river, to maintain a constant water level and to protect the city from high tides. The Weir has been an enormous success and has helped to breathe new life into the river and into the city itself. Boat tours exploring the River Lagan and Belfast Harbour, where

RMS Titanic was built, take visitors under the Queen Elizabeth Bridge, opened by HRH Queen Elizabeth II in 1967, and the Queen's Bridge, opened by Queen Victoria in 1849.

Public Art on the River Lagan

The regeneration of the River Lagan symbolises the re-generation of Belfast and this is celebrated in dramatic artwork found on the towpaths and walks along the river's banks. Bigfish needs no introduction. This huge 10 metre (33 feet) salmon, which celebrates the regeneration of the river, is the work of local sculptor, John Kindness. It holds a special place in the hearts of Belfast folk. A close-up examination of Bigfish reveals that the ceramic plates on its skin tell the history of Belfast. Further upstream is the equally impressive Thanksgiving Square sculpture, called Harmony of Belfast. Standing 19.5 metres high (64 feet), it depicts a girl standing on a globe and symbolises 'hope, aspiration and spirituality'.

Top: Bigfish.
Centre: Harmony of Belfast.
Left: Belfast waterfront today.

News Letter Building

This part of Belfast was heavily bombed during three devastating WWII air raids in April/May 1941 and many historic buildings were destroyed. Among those that survived is the News Letter Building, 1872, on Donegall Street. Its style is classic late Victorian Gothic, with rich floral decorations and profiles of literary men and women. It was formerly home to the *News Letter*, founded in 1737 and the oldest continuously published newspaper in the world. In 1776, the *News Letter*'s enterprising publishers intercepted the American Declaration of Independence, on its way from Philadelphia to London and printed its contents before it reached King and Parliament.

Top left: The city at night.
Top right: River traffic at night.
Left: Harmony of Belfast and the Queen's Bridge.
Below: The former News Letter Building, Donegall Street.

Merchant Hotel

The five-star Merchant Hotel occupies a magnificent Grade 1 listed property that was formerly the headquarters of the Ulster Bank. Completed in 1860, it is Italianate in style with stunning, classically styled interiors. Sculptures around the huge dome inside symbolise science, poetry, sculpture and music. It is one of the most renowned and best loved buildings in Belfast.

Right: Clarendon No. 1 Graving Dock.
Below: Graving Dock and lock gates.

Clarendon Dock

Clarendon Dock is the birthplace of ship building in Belfast and it played a pivotal role in the town's development as a great trading port. Between 1796–1800, a 76 metre (249 feet) long dry dock, Clarendon No. 1 Graving Dock was constructed, followed by a second dry dock, Clarendon No. 2 in 1826. Dock buildings comprise a long eight-bay sandstone workshop in the centre, with an engine house in basalt built across the east end, and a handsome two-storey dwelling house for the Dock Master at the west end. Both dry docks, together with the buildings, have been restored and they constitute a very important survival from the early days of the port of Belfast. In recent years, Clarendon Dock has undergone major redevelopment as part of the regeneration of the Laganside area. It has been transformed into a high quality environment for office and residential units. An impressive 8.3 metres (27 feet) high bronze sculpture, 'Dividers', stands near to Clarendon Docks Nos. 1 & 2.

Queen's Quarter

Queen's Quarter, centred round Queen's University and the beautiful Lanyon Building, is bursting with artistic creativity and is renowned for its entertainment and nightlife. It is also home to a treasure trove of fascinating shops and enticing restaurants and cafés. Queen's Quarter has some of the funkiest bars in the city, as well as live music and comedy venues and pubs with traditional Irish music sessions.

Much of the architectural heritage of Queen's Quarter dates from the Victorian period. The red brick and mellow sandstone of this style, found typically in the Lanyon Building, is softened by the numerous trees that thrive here, and together they lend Queen's Quarter its distinctive character.

Queen's Quarter has a lively calendar of cultural events throughout the year, culminating each autumn in the world-renowned Belfast Festival at Queen's, the largest festival of its kind in Ireland.

The Lanyon Building

Named after its architect, Charles Lanyon, the Lanyon Building is the centrepiece of Queen's University and one of the principal ornaments of Belfast. It was completed as Queen's College in 1849, the year Queen Victoria and Prince Albert made their only visit to Belfast, and became Queen's University in 1908.

In his design, Lanyon took inspiration from the Gothic and Tudor character of the great medieval universities of England. The central tower is an accurate translation of the Founder's Tower at Magdalen College, Oxford. The entrance hall has a great stained glass window designed by J.E. Nuttgens and installed after the Second World War. Doors lead out to the cloisters and quadrangle, and upstairs to the delightful Naughton Gallery, which features the University's art collection and touring exhibitions. The University's new Council Chamber and Canada Room, among the most popular of its reception venues, are also located on the first floor. The Queen's Welcome Centre, inside the front door, provides visitors and students with information about the university and what to do and see around Belfast.

The central quadrangle is the product of more than a century of building, yet it displays a remarkable degree of homogeneity. Only a short section of the south wing is part of the original design. The old Physics Building, with its tower and passageway, was designed by W.H. Lynn in 1911, and the north wing of the Lanyon Building was added in 1951. Later additions include the former Social Science Building, now the Peter Froggatt Centre, opened in 1966, and the Administration Building, constructed in the 1970s.

Above: The Lanyon Building's impressive entrance (right) and stained glass windows (left).
Below: The Lanyon Building at Queen's University.

Union Theological College

Above: Union Theological College.
Below: Friar's Bush Cemetery.

This building was established by the Presbyterian Church as a college for the training of its ministers. When it opened on 5 December 1853, its official name was 'the Presbyterian College, Belfast', or 'Assembly's College'. It became 'The Union Theological College of the Presbyterian Church in Ireland' in 1978.

The original front section of the building was designed by Charles Lanyon and was built of stone from Scrabo quarries in North Down, at a cost of £5,000. The South wing by Young & McKenzie was added in 1869; the North wing and Chapel in 1881, to plans by Lanyon's son John.

The College building played its part in the history of Northern Ireland when, from 1921 to 1932, it was the home of the Northern Ireland Parliament, before it moved to Stormont. The House of Commons met in the Library and the Senate in the Chapel. In addition, from 1941 to 1948, the Department of Finance occupied most of the building after its premises were partially destroyed by German bombing.

Friar's Bush Cemetery

Friar's Bush Cemetery is Belfast's most ancient burial ground. It occupies a site of just less than a hectare (circa 2 acres) beside the Ulster Museum, surrounding a low central mound. It is steeped in mystery and has fascinated generations of Belfast's citizens and historians alike. Some believe that the site may have been used in pre-Christian times. Others think it was linked with St Patrick (died AD 490), a theory that is partly supported by two unusual stones on the central mound of the graveyard. One, the mysterious 'Friar's Stone', bears the date AD 485; the other is a worn stone pillar that may have been part of an early church. However, it is known that Friar's Bush was used as a place of worship by the Catholic population of Belfast from the late 1600s until 1784.

During the major cholera epidemic of 1832 to 1833 Friar's Bush was used as a 'cholera pit'. The low grassy mound close to the entrance is still known as 'the Plaguey Hill'. It was re-opened in 1847 to receive typhus victims. Friar's Bush Cemetery finally closed in 1869. However, it is an important ecclesiastical site that pre-dates Belfast and it remains a revered place in the folk memory and traditions of its citizens.

Elmwood Hall

Formerly Elmwood Presbyterian Church, Elmwood Hall combines an eclectic mix of architectural styles into what has been described as 'a very pleasantly eccentric' church. It was built 1859-1862 to the design of a gifted amateur architect, John Corry, a director of the family firm of contractors and ship owners. He displayed an unusually exotic artistic ability in this fine High-Victorian church.

The exterior shows influences of Renaissance, Venetian, medieval, classical, Moorish and French styles that are absorbed together into a very elaborate Irish version of a North Italian Gothic church. Pink Scrabo sandstone was used to face the church, with yellow sandstone for the tower and three-tier spire. The building has been deconsecrated and is used as a concert hall.

Top left: The entrance to Friar's Bush Cemetery.
Top right: Elmwood Hall.
Bottom: Entrance to Elmwood Hall.

Botanic Gardens

This wonderful public garden, first established in 1828 by the Belfast Botanic and Horticultural Society, was sold to Belfast Corporation in 1895. Today the garden is a green lung in the heart of the city, and provides a focus for numerous public events throughout the year – from pop and classical concerts, to 'food-fests'. The Botanic Gardens contain two unique buildings – the Palm House and the Tropical Ravine, as well as the world renowned Ulster Museum.

PALM HOUSE AND TROPICAL RAVINE

The Palm House in Botanic Gardens, designed by Charles Lanyon, is one of the oldest surviving examples of a curvilinear iron and glass structure anywhere in the world. The foundation stone for the Palm House was laid on 22 June 1839 and the following year its two wings, each 23 metres (75 feet) long, 6 metres (20 feet) high and 6 metres (20 feet) wide, were completed at a cost of £1,400. They were the work of the renowned ironmaster, Richard Turner of Dublin and pre-date by some years his other great achievement, the Great Palm House at Kew (1844–1848). The 14 metres (46 feet) high el-

Top: Statue of Lord Kelvin, Botanic Gardens.
Centre: Inside the Palm House.
Bottom: The Palm House, Botanic Gardens.

liptical dome was added in 1852 by Young of Edinburgh, finally realising Lanyon's elegant and symmetrical design and providing space for the growing of lofty plants.

The Palm House epitomises the Victorian passion for horticulture, and over the years, it has acquired a reputation for exciting plant collections. The cool wing houses all-year-round displays of colour and scent using plants such as geranium, fuchsia, begonia and bulb displays. The hotter stove wing is a mini jungle of exotic plants, such as the striking bird of paradise, heavily scented frangipani and colourful bromeliads. The dome area contains a range of temperate and tropical plants.

Nearby is a second quirky and individualistic conservatory – the Tropical Ravine house, built by the head gardener and his staff, and finished in 1889. This rectangular building is uniquely constructed so that visitors can walk around a balcony and look down into a moist glen filled with tropical plants.

Top: The Ulster Museum.
Below: The curvilinear iron and glass of the Palm House, Botanic Gardens.

Ulster Museum

The Ulster Museum is the perfect place to take time out to explore art, ancient and modern history and the natural world. Visitors can see a rich variety of Irish and international fine and decorative arts, trace the story of the north of Ireland, its people and their achievements (including artefacts retrieved from the Spanish Armada vessel, *Girona*, which sank off the County Antrim coast in 1588), and explore the wonderful diversity of the natural world.

Charles Lanyon (1813–1889)

Belfast is sometimes referred to as 'Lanyon city'. This is hardly surprising, considering the incredible impact Charles Lanyon had on the architecture of the city. Born in Eastbourne, he moved to Dublin in the 1830s as a civil engineer to the Irish Board of Works. In time, he took up a civil engineering post in Antrim, where he was responsible for the construction of the coast road from Larne to Portrush, as well as the Belfast-Ballymena railway line. The Belfast-Bangor line in County Down and the Queen's and Ormeau bridges in Belfast can also be attributed to him.

However, it is in the field of architecture that he is perhaps best known. Having established his own architectural firm, from the 1840s on he designed and erected numerous buildings in Belfast, including Queen's College (now the Lanyon Building of Queen's University), the Crumlin Road Courthouse and Gaol, the Union Theological College in Botanic Avenue, the Palm House in Botanic Gardens. Other commissions were completed with his partner, William Henry Lynn: the Custom House, the Public Library in Royal Avenue and Belfast Castle.

He moved into politics in the 1860s, becoming Mayor of Belfast in 1862 and an MP for the borough in 1866. Knighted in 1868, he died in his house in Whiteabbey in 1889, and was buried in Newtownbreda churchyard.

Methodist College

Methodist College Belfast, or 'Methody' as it is popularly known, is one of Northern Ireland's leading grammar schools. It was founded in 1865, when Methodists in Ireland numbered only 23,000 out of a total population of 6 million. The decision was taken to build a college in Belfast for the training of Methodist ministers and as a school for boys. Three years later, on 18 August 1868, the College was opened with 141 pupils. Just after its opening, a proposal that 'young ladies' be educated on equal terms with the boys was accepted by the committee of management, so that from the third month of its existence, Methodist College has been a co-educational establishment. Methodist College comprises an attractive group of buildings in red Belfast brick with dressings of freestone from Glasgow, all on a base of Scrabo sandstone.

Above: Entrance to the Methodist College.
Below: Methodist College Belfast, or 'Methody'.

Shopping in Belfast

Queen's Quarter

When it comes to shopping, Queen's Quarter caters for mainstream tastes, as well as those who prefer a more eclectic retail experience. The Lisburn, Ormeau, Stranmillis Roads & Botanic Avenue are a shopping panacea – where one can find just about any gift required: unusual crafts, exquisite items for the home, designer label clothes & shoes, books, leather goods and quality antiques. And, for an especially 'tasteful' gift, there are wonderful delis and bespoke interior design stores. Visitors find that because many of the shops are privately owned, often with the owners serving their customers, they deliver an extra personal touch and a degree of exclusivity that makes shopping in Queen's Quarter a special experience in these days of anonymous, multi-national retail outlets.

Titanic Quarter

Titanic Quarter is one of the most exciting and prestigious waterfront developments in Europe, a multi-million pound focus for hi-tech business, residential and leisure activities. Yet historically, this Quarter of Belfast is steeped in shipbuilding. Its very skyline is dominated by the two enormous Harland and Wolff shipyard cranes, Goliath and Samson, symbols of the engineering genius that gave birth to some of the mightiest vessels ever to set sail.

Perhaps the name most closely associated with Harland and Wolff is that of *RMS Titanic*, the ill-fated liner built for the White Star Line and the largest moving object of its day, which sank so tragically in 1912. Titanic Quarter takes its name from this mighty vessel. Visitors can discover much about this ship, and the people who made her, as they explore Titanic Quarter.

Above: One of the huge Harland & Wolff gantry cranes.
Below: The Thompson Graving Dock.

Above: Titanic Quarter, home to RMS Titanic.
Below: Harland & Wolff buildings in Titanic Quarter.

Harland & Wolff created two larger slipways to accommodate the new liners. A massive framework of Arrol Gantry was constructed, which remained a landmark of Belfast Harbour for nearly seventy years.

In 1918 the company opened its East Yard, which specialised in mass-produced ships of standard design. This brought the payroll up to 22,000 men. The shipyard played a vital role for the Allies during World War II, building 6 aircraft carriers, 2 cruisers and 131 other naval ships, and repairing over 22,000 other vessels. It also manufactured tanks and artillery components and the workforce peaked at around 35,000 during this time. With the rise of air travel in the 1950s, demand for passenger ships declined. The last cruiser built by the yard was *RMS Canberra* in 1960.

Today Harland & Wolff has refocused its operations into a project management organisation, specialising in design and structural engineering, as well as ship repair and offshore construction.

Thompson Graving Dock

When the Thompson Graving Dock opened in 1911, it was the largest dry dock in the world, the only one capable of holding the Olympic-class liners, *Olympic*, *Titanic* and *Britannic*. The vessels were fitted-out with everything required for the operation of a great hotel and a great ocean liner. The three 1,000 horse-power pumping engines in the Thompson Pump House, beside the dry dock, could drain all 105 million litres (23 million gallons) of water from the full dock in around 100 minutes.

The Harland & Wolff Shipyard

The partnership of Edward Harland and Gustav Wolff laid the foundations for what was to become one of the greatest shipyards in the world. Belfast's first iron shipbuilding yard was opened by Robert Hickson in 1853. In December 1854, he employed Edward Harland as general manager. Harland purchased the business from Hickson for £5,000 in 1858 and Edward James Harland & Co. opened for business. Three years later, in 1861, he went into partnership with his personal assistant, Gustav Wilhelm Wolff. Harland & Wolff had been formed.

A pivotal figure entered the Harland & Wolff story in 1862. Aged just fifteen years, William James Pirrie joined the company as a 'gentleman apprentice'. An excellent draughtsman, he was made a partner in 1874, at the age of twenty-seven. When Harland died in 1894, Pirrie became Chairman of the company, a position he held until his death in 1924. Under his management, Harland & Wolff experienced unprecedented growth. In 1854 the yard employed 100 men, by 1897 it employed 10,000.

In 1870 Harland & Wolff built *Oceanic*, the first of over seventy vessels the yard was to build for the White Star Line. The most famous of these were the trio of Olympic-class vessels, *Olympic*, *Titanic* and *Britannic*. Devised by Pirrie and Bruce Ismay, Chairman of the White Star Line, they were designed and built at Harland & Wolff between 1908 and 1914.

Drawing Offices

The Harland and Wolff Drawing Offices are housed in two buildings attached to the rear of the main Harland and Wolff Headquarters Building. This is where the detailed construction designs for the Olympic-class liners *Olympic*, *Titanic* and *Britannic* were drawn. They have ornately decorated, high vaulted ceilings, inset with large fanlights to flood the rooms below with natural light and are amongst the oldest remaining sections of the company's buildings in Titanic Quarter.

Goliath and Samson

These two massive yellow cranes, situated in Harland & Wolff's Queen's Island shipyard, are distinctive features of the Belfast skyline and landmark structures of the city. The first crane to be built, known as Goliath, was completed in 1969, and the second crane, Samson, was completed in 1974. They are now scheduled as historic monuments, although both are still used for ship repair and other engineering projects.

Olympic and Titanic Slipways

Slips No. 2 and 3 are where the White Star Liners *Olympic* and *Titanic* were built. Although quiet and peaceful today, in 1910 this entire area was a hive of human industry, reverberating to the deafening din from steel plates being hammered and riveted and from the belching of mighty steam cranes at the Harland & Wolff shipyard. A massive gantry, constructed by Sir William Arrol & Company of Glasgow, stood like a geometric spider's web around the hulls of *Olympic* and *Titanic* on the slips. The gantry, measuring 256 metres (840 feet) long and 82 metres (270 feet) wide and reaching up to 69 metres (228 feet) at its tallest point, remained in use at Harland and Wolff until the 1960s.

Above: The Thompson Pump House.
Below: The twin gantry cranes, Samson and Goliath, at twilight.

HMS Caroline

The Alexandra Graving Dock holds a significant piece of maritime history. *HMS Caroline* is a World War One light cruiser and the second oldest commissioned warship in the Royal Navy (the

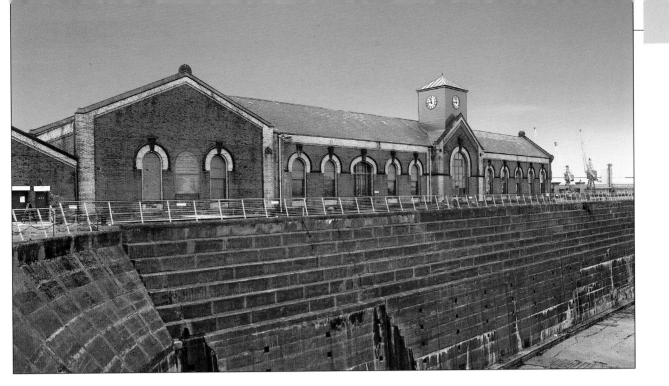

oldest being *HMS Victory*). The ship currently serves as Headquarters for the Ulster Division, Royal Navy Reserve. Launched in September 1914, she served in the North Sea throughout WWI and saw action in the Battle of Jutland, fought between the British Grand Fleet and the German High Seas Fleet in May 1916. This was the largest surface naval battle of the metal ship era and the only major fleet action of World War One. She is believed to be the sole survivor of that great action. Today *HMS Caroline* is listed on the National Historic Ships Register, thereby protecting her for future generations. She is expected to serve in her current role for the foreseeable future.

Titanic Slipway

On 31 May 1911, *SS 401. Titanic* slid down Slipway No. 3 at the Queen's Yard of Harland & Wolff and settled on the waters of the Victoria Channel in Belfast Lough. In her brief life she would be the largest, most luxurious vessel ever built.

Titanic was the product of a contract to build three massive ships that had been awarded to Harland & Wolff by the White Star Line of Liverpool in July 1908. The Chief Designer and Managing Director, Thomas Andrews, was closely involved with the design and construction of the new Olympic-class vessels. Following her successful sea trials, *Titanic* left Belfast, arriving at Southampton just after midnight on 4 April 1912, from where she departed on her first trans-Atlantic crossing to New York. At 11.40pm on Sunday, 14 April 1912, while travelling at a speed approaching 22 knots, *Titanic* struck an iceberg. At 12.25am Captain Smith realised the ship was lost and gave the order to start filling lifeboats – 'women and children first'. At 2.19am the ship split in two between the second and third funnels, and by 2.20am, two hours and forty minutes after striking the iceberg, *RMS Titanic*

Above: Thompson Graving Dock and Thompson Pump House, Titanic Quarter.
Below: HMS Caroline.

slipped into the sea and began its descent to the ocean floor. The tragedy of the *Titanic* and the loss of 1,522 souls, is commemorated in a beautiful and moving monument by Sir Thomas Brock which stands in the grounds of Belfast City Hall.

Out and About

North Belfast

By the mid and late 1800s, North Belfast, and the Antrim Road in particular, had the most desirable residential addresses in Belfast, home to wealthy bankers, merchants and shipping magnates. Some houses in the area even had turret towers, so that the ship-owner residents could supervise the arrival and departure of their vessels. Its status was further enhanced in 1870, when the third Marquis of Donegall built Belfast Castle.

BELFAST CASTLE
The third Marquis of Donegall engaged the Belfast firm of Lanyon, Lynn and Lanyon to design this large, Scottish Baronial style mansion, which commands magnificent views of Belfast Lough and the city from its prominent site on the slopes of Cave Hill. Completed in 1870, it was presented to Belfast Corporation in 1934. The Castle is open to the public and is a popular venue for weddings and functions.

BELFAST ZOO AND CAVE HILL
Belfast Zoo is home to over 160 species of wild animals. Its award-winning enclosures recreate many natural habitats and it has an international reputation for its success in breeding, particularly with endangered species. Belfast Zoo extends almost to the top of the Cave Hill, which rises to 360 metres (1,182 feet) above sea level and is steeped in over 3,000 years of history. It has a Stone Age cairn, Neolithic forts and caves that reputedly hid highwaymen. The summit offers breath-taking panoramas across County Down.

Above: Belfast Zoo and Cave Hill.
Below: The County Court building, Crumlin Road.

CRUMLIN ROAD GAOL
This imposing and sinister building was designed by the renowned architect Sir Charles Lanyon and completed in 1846, at a cost of £60,000. Now a Grade A listed building, the Gaol is an outstanding example of Victorian penal architecture and planning. It has four wings that radiate in a fan-shape from a central hall known as the Circle. It was the first prison in Ireland to be designed for 'The Separate System' of confinement, whereby prisoners were permanently separated from each other, and never allowed to meet or converse. During the 150 years that it remained in use, 17 men were executed and their bodies buried within the prison walls. Opposite the Gaol stands the County Courthouse, completed in 1850 to designs by Lanyon. An underground tunnel links the Gaol to the Courthouse.

Shankill

Shankill is perhaps synonymous with the Shankill Road, a name which featured prominently in news bulletins for many years. However, it is in fact an ancient land and its first settlers lived in earthworks known as raths, or ring forts. Seven of these circular defensive structures dating from around AD 400 have been located in the area.

SHANKILL GRAVEYARD
Shankill Graveyard reveals much about the social and economic development of Belfast. It is one of the most

intriguing archaeological sites in the city. Tradition has it that Saint Patrick founded a church here some time around the fifth century. This graveyard was the final resting place for the rich and poor alike, including Alexander Craig (died 1861), Deputy Harbour Master for Belfast, whose headstone reads:

Who for 79 years weathered the Battle and the Breeze and now lies here one fathom deep.

St Matthew's Parish Church

The daring originality of St Matthew's, the shape of which is based on the ancient Orthodox churches of Greece and Asia Minor, makes it stand out from other less adventurous Victorian places of worship. From its smooth coved ceilings, to the superb brickwork of its exterior, St Matthew's Parish Church is a truly remarkable creation.

East Belfast

During the nineteenth century, as Belfast grew and prospered, the east of the town emerged as a thriving industrial heartland. There were shipyards, mills and rope works employing thousands of workers. At its height for example, the Belfast Ropeworks Company Limited was the world's largest manufacturer of rope and twine. It supplied over one-third of all the Allied Forces' requirements for rope during WWII. The Ropeworks closed in 1983. The mighty Harland & Wolff shipyard was equally successful, launching over 2,000 ships in its history, including the ill-fated *RMS Titanic*.

Parliament Buildings, Stormont Estate

Parliament Buildings is one of the most outstanding architectural sights in Ireland. Elegant and dignified, it is approached by a long processional avenue and occupies a beautifully landscaped site cut into rising ground, framed

C. S. Lewis

One of the city's most famous literary sons, the author C. S. Lewis (1898–1963) was born in Strandtown in East Belfast. Lewis is perhaps best known for his fictional series, *The Chronicles of Narnia*, but he wrote many other works on medieval literature, Christian apologetics and literary criticism. He is celebrated in the life-size statue, *The Searcher*, by sculptor Ross Wilson, unveiled at Holywood Arches in 1998.

by mature trees and broad lawns. It was constructed to accommodate the newly formed Government of Northern Ireland, established under the Government of Ireland Act, 1920. Work started in March 1923 and the building was declared open on 16 November 1932. It served as the seat of the Parliament of Northern Ireland for forty years until 1972 when, following political unrest, Northern Ireland came under direct rule from the Westminster Parliament. It is now the home of the Northern Ireland Assembly, which has operated from the building since 1998.

Above: C. S. Lewis.
Below: Parliament Buildings, Stormont Estate.

South Belfast

In the 1600s this area of South Belfast was covered by a wild and dangerous forest of oak and elm trees that was inhabited by wolves. Yet in 1871, Belfast Corporation opened Ormeau Park as the first public park in Belfast. It remains a green oasis for visitors, and its original Victorian bandstand is still in place. The parklands incorporate Ormeau Golf Club, formed in 1893, and one of the oldest Golf Clubs in Ireland.

Ballynafeigh Methodist Church, on the Ormeau Road, is a fine example of a preaching church and offers an interesting, if eccentric, interior. Completed in 1899, it is a delightful adaptation of an Elizabethan theatre. Its curved gallery and fretwork roof are held aloft on high wooden columns, and a circular seating system, with the pulpit at its centre, allows every person an uninterrupted view of the speaker. This layout was much favoured by John Wesley, the early leader of the Methodist movement.

Above: The Bandstand, Ormeau Park.
Below: Murals, the Falls Road, West Belfast.

Gaeltacht Quarter, West Belfast

A former Presbyterian church on the Falls Road is an unlikely location for Belfast's only Irish language arts and culture centre, but it is home to Cultúrlann Mc Adam Ó Fiaich, the hub of the city's vibrant and fast growing Irish language community. The Gaeltacht Quarter comprises the communities of the Falls Road. Their rich and vibrant culture combines Irish language, dancing and music. These are showcased in programmes of activities by Féile an Phobail, culminating in the annual festival, August Féile.

The Falls Road (always called *the* Falls Road) takes its name from the Irish, *Bóthar na bhFál*, meaning 'road of the hedgerows'. As this name implies, it was originally a country lane leading from the cen-

St Peter's Cathedral

St Peter's is the mother church of the Diocese of Down & Connor, and was the first Catholic Church in Belfast to be built in the Gothic style. The ground on which it stands was donated by Barney Hughes, a successful local baker and renowned philanthropist. Fr Jeremiah Ryan McAuley, who trained as an architect before he was ordained, designed the building. It opened on Sunday, 14 October 1866 and the distinction of Cathedral was conferred on 29 June 1986.

Above: Royal Victoria Hospital.
Right: St Peter's Cathedral, West Belfast.

tre of Belfast. However, with rising industrialisation and the growth of linen mills in the nineteenth century, the population expanded rapidly and a network of narrow streets with back-to-back terrace housing was built to accommodate the mill workers. A tour of the Conway Mill, built around 1840, reveals the harsh, wet conditions that mill workers had to endure.

Royal Victoria Hospital

The Royal Victoria Hospital, commonly known as 'The Royal' or the 'RVH', is a landmark building on the Falls Road. Built between 1900 and 1903, it represented a revolution in hospital design, with single-storey wards placed compactly side by side throughout. It is also believed to be the first ever building to have installed air conditioning for human comfort. Today 'The Royal' is made up of four linked hospitals – the Royal Victoria, Royal Jubilee Maternity Service, Royal Belfast Hospital for Sick Children and the Dental Hospital.

One of the most interesting and unusual visitor attractions to have risen to prominence in recent years is Northern Ireland's murals. Over 2,000 wall paintings have been documented in its towns and cities since the 1970s. The painting of murals has involved both the Protestant/Loyalist and Nationalist/Republican communities and the artwork frequently reflects one side's political point of view. Some of the harder-edged militaristic murals are now being transformed into softer works depicting local heroes, such as football legend, George Best, or historic events, such as the Irish Famine.

In Belfast, there are taxi and open-top bus tours of the murals. Contact the Belfast Welcome Centre in the City Centre for full details.

Above: Nationalist/Republican murals.
Below: Loyalist murals.

There are great days away to be enjoyed within a short drive of Belfast. Whatever one's age or interest, Northern Ireland is full of amazing things to do, awe inspiring sights to see and fascinating places to explore. From the relaxing to the physically demanding; educational to thought provoking, visitors will be spoilt for choice and fully entertained with some truly memorable days out.

Ulster Folk & Transport Museum

The folk museum tells the story of Ulster's past through buildings that have been saved and meticulously reconstructed on this 27 hectare (60 acres) site. Cottages, schools, a church, water-powered mill and other buildings vividly recreate early twentieth-century life in the north of Ireland. There is also a comprehensive transport collection, from horse-drawn carts to Irish-built motor cars, including the exotic but ill-fated DeLorean gull-wing DMC car.

Main page: The Giant's Causeway.
Insets: Ulster Folk & Transport Museum.

Causeway Coast and Giant's Causeway

The Causeway Coastal Route has been rated as one of the Top Five Road Trips worldwide. It hugs the narrow strip of coastline that runs between the sea and high cliffs from Carrickfergus to Portrush, and is perfect for a leisurely tour. The route is a gateway to the Nine Glens of Antrim – Glenarm, Glencloy, Glenariff, Glenballyemon, Glencorp, Glenaan, Glendun, Glenshesk and Glentaisie. Catch the narrow gauge steam train from Bushmills to Northern Ireland's most famous attraction, the Giant's Causeway. Formed some 62 to 65 million years ago, it is an awe-inspiring landscape of basalt columns.

Mourne Mountains

The Mournes are a very compact range of mountains. Immortalised in a poignant song by Percy French, 'Where the Mountains of Mourne sweep down to the sea', they are also said to have been the inspiration for C. S. Lewis's Kingdom of Narnia. Their rugged peaks, criss-crossed by dry stone walls, offer wonderful walks with superb scenery. Serious hikers may wish to follow the Mourne Wall along its 35.4 kilometres (22 miles), as it runs like a roller coaster from peak to peak.

Right: Hexagonal rock formations at the Giant's Causeway.
Below: The Mountains of Mourne, County Down.

Distributed by
The O'Brien Press Ltd., 12 Terenure Road East, Rathgar, Dublin 6, Ireland
Tel. +353 1 4923333; Fax +353 1 4922777
e-mail: books@obrien.ie; Website: www.obrien.ie
ISBN 978-1-84717-150-4
First published 2009

© Copyright 2009 by Casa Editrice Bonechi - Florence - Italy
Tel. +39 055576841 - Fax +39 0555000766
e-mail: bonechi@bonechi.it - Internet: www.bonechi.com
ISBN 978-88-476-2449-8

Publication created by Casa Editrice Bonechi. *Publication Manager:* Monica Bonechi
Photographic research: Editorial Staff of Casa Editrice Bonechi
Graphic design, layout: Alessandro Calonego, Elena Nannucci
Cover: Elena Nannucci. *Editing:* Patrizia Fabbri, Síne Quinn. *Texts by* Alan Morrow

Printed in Italy by Centro Stampa Editoriale Bonechi.

PHOTOGRAPHY ACKNOWLEDGMENTS
Photographs from archives of Casa Editrice Bonechi *taken by* Andrea Fantauzzo,
Ghigo Roli *(page 20 above).*

Other contributors:
Photographs pages 60 above, 61 above: © Fáilte Feirste Thiar.

*The publisher apologises for any omissions and is willing to make amends with the formal recognition
of the author of any photo subsequently identified.*

* * *